I0298460

Your Person Doesn't Belong To You

Your Person Doesn't Belong To You

Isabel Sobral Campos

Vegetarian Alcoholic Press

Published in the United States by Vegetarian Alcoholic Press.

For Kris & Otília

Acknowledgements

Thanks to the following journals, where versions of some these poems were previously published: *Tammy* ("A Dream," "30 May 1431," "Jeanne d'Arc to Carl Dreyer") and *Small Po[r]tions* ("Eros," "Bone Diary"). Thanks also to dancing girl press for publishing my chapbook *You Will Be Made of Stone.*

I am especially grateful to Joshua Loveless, Adrian Kien, and Joseph Massey for carefully reading early versions of this manuscript and offering invaluable insight. Freddy La Force's dedication to Vegetarian Alcoholic Press is truly unique and I am thrilled be a small part of it.

A special thanks to my partner Kristofer J. Petersen-Overton for reading *Your Person Doesn't Belong To You* many times and for all his loving care, suggestions, and support. To my darling daughter Otília, my sisters Inês and Rita, and my parents Celeste and Rui, all my love.

Finally, I am very grateful to Anselm Berrigan for publishing "Biography" in the *Brooklyn Rail,* for reading the full manuscript and, most of all, for being such an inspiring writer and teacher.

Contents

Jeanne d'Arc was only nineteen years old when she was burned at the stake in the city of Rouen on May 30, 1431. After months of interrogation by an Inquisition court, she agreed to forego her preference for men's clothing and publicly recanted her visions of St. Margaret, St. Catherine, and St. Michael. For this, the Maid of Orléans was initially spared death and instead condemned to perpetual imprisonment. But on May 28, after learning that she had once again donned a soldier's garb, the judges confronted Jeanne in her cell. Her concessions, she told them, had been a mistake and she withdrew her earlier recantation.

In 1928, Carl Dreyer directed a film about Jeanne d'Arc, *La Passion de Jeanne d'Arc*. This fragmented and discontinuous work relies on transcripts of the historical trial and features repeated and prolonged close-up shots of Jeanne's face, famously played by Renée Jeanne Falconetti. Two fires in different cities destroyed original versions of the film. It was presumed lost until 1981, when an employee of a mental institution in Oslo discovered yet another version of the original stored in canisters within a janitor's closet.

"I'm the fragment of your thought,
facet of your hallucination."

Jeanne d'Arc to Carl Dreyer

Understanding

is a madrigal sinking in the marsh
one comes to doubt the sun

The afternoon reeks of thought,
I won't speak of nights: blank like ice begging some soothing

I test these tentacles, the gardened
warp of minutes,

lamps gyring oblivion
What I know from
looking at this grille of time:

banners make wonderful belts worms stupendous earrings

Then wet fog
under enforced skirts

clings to the open
pit between my legs

Fog roams wetting
my dried interior
blowing up the skirt's
dimension into a single
alien curve,

the sagging drip of
its wetness on the
weighted hair

Drowning

me already in
swampy
earthiness

I tear the skirt
The fog gales up
with fossil smell

I'm beginning

to think

like a fish,

a mutant minnow.

La Passion de Jeanne d'Arc
Intertitle 3:12

Une jeune femme qui
mourut pour son pays

Dulce et decorum est pro patria mori.

"Militarism is the compulsory, universal use of violence as a means to the ends of the state."

What I know extends
beyond liquid daylight

Observe the woman eating grass
spitting into mouths of children

Someone may want to know
what birds we killed to
satiate this hunger What measures
beyond observation: she wraps herself

in her sylvan skirts. Cups her hands to
the poisoned well.

Her fingernails scratch late spring snow

searching
the twig of life

This one-eyed blackness   through cracks in vision
I see and rejoice in shadows This   my hiding place
in a cell's curvature, the barred chiaroscuro

It's true

the cockroach is God,

my crumbs are offerings

The mouse requests a single ear canal
in which to sleep

Inside unmarked hours   of a bare calendar

what I know escapee of feelers does not compound
to any unity I hurl these fragments against myself

the summoning of orbits   speaking to the ghost

of fathers   within division of things

La Passion de Jeanne d'Arc
sixth minute

Although I'm not averse to conceding the power of the object. Although I can be swept by incantations as much as the next person. The Lord's prayer is as strange as a spatula becoming conduit for otherworldly spirits. Or accepting the wind really carries voices of the dead as my grandmother used to say. Or surmising that I die inside my life and live inside my death. Jeanne points to the MOTHER as the site and birth of the tragic in the sixth minute at frames 36 to 44 seconds.

If I know

liquescent blush

The horse I rode becomes   my face stamped into his

veins,

I come to smell of manure and gallop when
asked to stand   "spongy kneecaps" I say,   if they knew

my punctured wounds won't heal unless   they salivate

I'm a tongue-tied horse

La Passion de Jeanne d'Arc
Intertitle 7:03

And the father becomes the cross, *"Voulez-vous réciter le Pater?"*

Non, non, non, non, non, non, non, non, non

A peace emblem grows inaudible

My appearance as stallion gait
    is still ambush,   when you
bat an eye, here   I advance

    Now memory floppy as a rag doll
and just as promiscuous   The red armor

    in steeled glitter   I know that

I will find the nothing
    at the end of this road:
my drowned reflection   sunk in the belly of fish

    I will find a slow digestion   What I know is crude

a dream of cosseted weeds   unprepared for osmatic fire

If a fluttering fist says all

If
    a show of force contradicts

Even I know
    There is no victory

I used to sit between eggs,   thinking,

around me the sun
    corroded udders

    If,   espied below the mountain one finds
a strange glowing solution that chooses us

    Sarcophagi   suggested

Not if, a glowing triad illuminated my name

    At times there is only banality
Of a body that thirsts, hungers, defecates
    In the pure banality still
    Only what counts
The body that thirsts, hungers, defecates
    The medium of prophecy
    An eelpout   chokehold

I slept wrapped in meat thinking

    about the face
    you carry now

La Passion de Jeanne d'Arc
Intertitle 11:06

Pourquoi avez-vous pris cet habit d'homme?

Pourquoi

d'homme?

habit

Est-ce que vous

voulez être un homme?

hommes

plus que les femmes?

Aimez-vous les

Not as long as mountains sleep
in the watchfulness of wolves
will I dream again

For the world dreams
in my stead
these common cycles
They appear and disappear
Fort-da,
Fort-da,
Fort-da!
Not as long as
I've forgotten the names of childhood birds

Let them
remain hidden

For these wonders
are now cloudbursts

in my brain
I lay solitary

chained
to the morning sun

No, I know this:
Someone will count the steps from the left to the right
Wall in this solitary
Cell
Of false penitents

I refused to walk
My horse won't heed me
The canebrakes won't beat me
The wishbone won't catch me
The crossbow won't hunt me
…
…
…
…
…
…
…
…
…

Les autres femmes washing their smoky hair

Against a quartered sky
      I begin to know   how much I wished   to wring their hair

My muggy *belles*   I dive fishy   Every
      time they stretch their necks at the mallards

As if in ancient recognition of their inward sparrows

      Before you cut my veins
      their shadowed curls will
wave like that many
      fungible fingers

      All this flickers like a lost limb when I look
      through the slit
shackled   the half-moonlight hurts

Sometimes understanding is unfilled
  Not even outline

That zero of zeroes
  unoccupied
before words

  I hate to dream
  I expect to find a rope at the cusp of consciousness

  The blade And its evasion So my death won't be whole

I expect the world eclipsed in the nape of the moon
  I have trouble facing light

  In the paraphernalia of prisons   I exist
incrusted in lianas upending walls

  I exist nameless in a breathless coop
Feathered by grace

La Passion de Jeanne d'Arc
Intertitle 31:17

Non Non Non Non Non Non Non, non, non, non, non, non, non, non, non

It's true:

They come every morning
Their old skin and rubbed moles

Their wrinkled noses and desiccated lips
Their shrouded lust

They want my manliness to seep out: the entrails of a sacrificial fish

The entrails of a cottontail
The scar tissue of an old horse
The blood on the wolfhound maw

They want to untie my pants
the show of a bare (wo)man leg
shaking hot pincers with their trembling hands

Their ooze of coal heat

The cave hidden below cool with its ice
hides me

I untie my pants   A warm whiff of summer

Bouts of silence

And my horse licks invisible
His flaccid tongue, approaches   almost I see
what he wants   a tap on his sun-warmed flank

They ask what I eat
I fast all the wet corn they give me
The wolf-spider's thaw

You can't feed me
You can't give me food to eat

The deathly motion of monument

You will be made of stone

A hat or a bonnet on that figure

You will not feel or know it

The era begins again

You will not know your relevance

I wish I could read and write my name

Your name will mean nothing

Something will be extinguished

Fascists will claim you

This voice is not an oracle of myself

You don't know what you hear or feel

I betrayed the call of angels

Better dead than killing

They will carve the flowing hair I have renounced

Your person doesn't belong to you

I fought against tyranny, I was tyranny

You questioned war too late

I thought of the horse, I became the horse

The horse doesn't need you

The statue will be gray

The statue will be bombed

The statue will be a painting

The statue will be a film

The statue will live

The statue will haunt you

I will wake up at the end

You believed in war, don't you understand?

A dent in history

This planet's demise

I wanted the man inside the woman

Poor excuse, besides

The man, the woman don't exist

I'll renounce my horse, I'll renounce my hut

Your loving horse won't renounce you

I'll forage, feeding off green

With the sheep that used to know me

You can't castoff your visions

They were saints who said saintly things

They were weapons, they carried blood

I didn't consider the other battle

Always visible instigating distance

I wanted peace with a horse

You wanted the book but couldn't read

Periwinkles on my dead face

Buttercups on your dead face

Larkspur on my dead face

And roses

Those were false visions

I'll crush the stone that I'll become

Not granite, not marble, not schist

The statue is made of clay

Not bronze, not alabaster

The statue is made of augury

Terracotta and chicken wire

All these terrifying epochs

When time holds still

So many, so much

Simply men or women

The lung, which is a wing

An appendage, it will burn

My heart and shoulder blade

Combustibles

Like gulls on my stone

They're eyeing leopards

Doves on my stone

They're slaying leopards

Partridge on my stone

Tomorrow in its rosy dawn

Because I chose my only choice

All dogs barked at midnight

Howling through sheets of fire

That fire that sticks like glue

Lynxes and oxen

Godly and ungodly

My horse and his sleeping mule

Geese in folded midnights

A clock that always stops

Inside the house where you were born

By the fire that warmed me

And the spoon that fed you

On the boat that led me

And the shoes that grounded you

A century and then another

When so much is irretrievable

My immortality is your death

Biscuits and bread

Onion and carrot

Beans and apples

A prohibition then fasting

Your mother already knew

This time of stone and steel

Like an insect knows

A ladder to climb unseen

Your mother was a dormant scholar

She knew of many things

With her slow disappearance

An image drawn with water

My face rubs against the cold stone

It knows something separate
from me

My face isn't my face as mine

It isn't a name
It's a color
shaped like a mountain
A valley, a river   a tree

Tuff   or grass
Cannibal   or clouded ash

A vent   citadel

turret
or cloak

My face is a
singing horse
wrapped in
a poor shawl

O it's stripped
O unrecognizable
A whorl on the bark

through the bars
my face is exterior

La Passion de Jeanne d'Arc
Intertitle 28:00

A fly on Falconetti's face, not Jeanne's

Sometimes knowing comes in gusts
Its soft pod looms like a dream

I don't want to know
more than the content of a day
or its luminous lining

How can I bargain for my life?
Lily pad on my still living body
Immobile in a living-death

I like to listen
I'll chew on air

La Passion de Jeanne d'Arc
Intertitle 1:16

Like a stone stays a corpse stares

Carnivorous

words fall from their holes

in trees

Owls dispense shrieks
survivor's moans

Telepathy
between
the condemned

I soap my face with light
in these bones without masks
Reverting the shadow's weight

Whether
    one sees it or not

knowledge
    is a catalyst

    of fire,
    a flammable.

    Windmills spin
    Fishhooks whirl
Tails define
    Because "whether" is a crossroad within thought
    The place that shifts when one decides to shift
An interrogation:
    Will you wear these womanly clothes?

Whether I feel the redwood glean in twilights
I've never been to this end of the world
And will not return without its insight
A wing in this dungeon I see
Whether I want or not
A spayed storm
    Continues

    My hands shake off minutes as I focus:
On releasing their shrouds   Their bulging divinity
And in the saga the past collides with its shadow

    Whether the root boils to a crust   or not   the root

will warble like a summer morning

    The absent root I crave   for some things   are too close to God namely,   roots   wheat   fountains

so they call me the shaman witch   my time

before Macbeth was dreamt

Whether they know it or not I'm dual sexed nature, and sometimes

(as I said)

my mind feels circular

like a fish's   returns without returning

A crippled light
Of women with women to women
Spreading mud to shelter the crotch
Who throw rocks at borders
And hide contraband under skirts
And use slingshots instead of crow's paws

Root of hemlock, gall of goat,
Scale of dragon, tooth of wolf

Whether the river's spells are real
their quest is material

I'm the either/or of their knowledge

That paradox of understanding that lures
In the end of answers
At the cusp of everything
I'm this wild woman

Some

poems

begin

by howling

Conversation - ···· ·-· --- ··- --· ···· a Peephole
(Morse Code)

··· ···· · ·-·· ·-··

··- ···
··- ···

I -·-· ·- -· hear you better with

- ···· ·   ··· -·- -·--

my left ear

·-   --· ·-· · -·--
··· ···· · ·-·· ·-··

where I curl like a mouse
-·-· ·- - ·- -·-· --- -- -···

inside a rough dent

·· -· ··· ·· -·· ·   --- ·-·   ·--· · ·-· ···· ·- ·--· ···
-·--· ·-   -·-· ·- - ·- -·-· --- -- -··· -·--·-

·-- ···· · ·-· ·   ··   ··· ·-·· · · ·--·
··   ·- --   ···· · ·-· ·

The wind blows like white

Hello,
green
sky

One hundred stars on the cusp of balancing but who looks up?

- .... .   -... --- .- -

A boat floats backward like a toppled umbrella

The boat   voice one:

.-   -.-. --- ..-. ..-. .. -.   and its pigmented

sound,

here   .- --. .- .. -.

- .... .   -... --- .- -

A woman inside the   as if inside a
(coffin)   .-   -.-. --- ..-. ..-. .. -.

a birdcage
without bars   .- ..-. - . .-. .-.. .. ..-. .
the (afterlife)
.- ..-. - . .-. .-.. .. ..-. .

.- ..-. - . .-. .-.. .. ..-. .

I was going to sleep but began thinking

- .... .. -. -.- .. -. --.

-... --- .- -

thinking

- .... .. -. -.- .. -. --.

dash dot dot dot dot dot dash dot dash dot dash dot dot

.-   -. ..- -. ...   .-- .. -- .--. .-.. .

.-.. .. -.- .   .- -.   --- .-- .-.. ...   .- -.. .

- .... .. -. -.- .. -. --.

... - .-. .- -. --. . .-.. -.--   .. -.   .-- .. -. - . .-.   .-- .- - -.-. ....

-.. .- ... .   -.. --- -   -.. --- -   -.. --- -   -.. --- -   -.. --- -   -.. .- ... .   -.. --- -
.-- .- - -.-. ....
-.. .- ... .   -.. --- -   -.. .- ... .   -.. --- -   -.. --- -   -.. .- ... .   -.. --- -   -.. .- ... .

-.. .- ... .   -.. --- -

A boat floats

~~my second~~ -.-   Blank

face in its cusp

one hundred stars

watch

who looks up?

Staring at the wall

A cortege of singing birds and sometimes VOICE TWO
on the other side where I suspect a bandit like me sleeps

-.. --- -   --. .   .-.. .. -.-. .   -.-- --- ..-

waiting for time watching with my starlight eye

..-. .. .-. .

... - .- - .. -.-.   the other has since become hooked on heat

... - .- - .. -.-.   i.e. (fire)

voice two: dot

-.. --- - me ME

from the afterlife

--.

--.

--.

--.

ME

ME

in my toxic sleep

Remote like a broken
bottle at the edge of a

cliff

peering
through a window
at a vacating

morning
your dash
to my dot
.. .. -.. --- - .
-.. --- - . --- -. --- -. -.-- --- ..- .-.
-.-- --- ..- .-. ...- --- .. -.-. . ...- --- .. -.-. .

... -. --- .-- -... ..- -.. ... .. -. -.-. --. --- -.

-.-- . - (yet)

nothing
happens

That a slug is golden like a peach

.- -. .. -- .- .-.. ...

A southern bestiary
of newly invented

(animals)

Look at

-- .

ME

-- .
-- .

through .--. . . .--. .... --- .-.. this
secular peephole

.. -- ... .--. . -. -
... .--. . -. -

- .... . .-- .. -.. --- .-- .- -.. ...- .- -. -.-. . ...
-.-- --- ..- .-. ..-. .- -.-. .
.. - .-- .. .-.. .-.. .-. .. .--. - .... . . -.-- . ... --- ..-. ..-.

VOICE
the dot-
fallacy of
but something too knobby

-.- -. --- -... -... -.--

TWO, not
dash
yesterday
for thought

In this high night's fever

.-- .... .- .-.. .

~~TAKE this word~~

to your gallows grave

...- --- .. -.-. .   --- -. . ..--..

VOICE ONE?

Dash me your oblique hello

A sleeping peephole hurts

..   ..   .- --   .-- --   - .... .. -. -.- .. -. --.   --- ..-.   --- ..-.   -.-- --- ..- .-.

- .... .. -. -.- .. -. --.

-.. .-. . .- -- .. -. --.

-.. .-. . .- -- .. -. --.

Sometimes you become a howl

A HOWL

.- .... --- .-- .-..

inside this small chest of roses

A place of deafness

.... --- .-- .-.. .. -. --.

You look at your feet without shoes

You look at your hands

Your howl is its own form of B-A-I-T

Like an afterbirth caught in the branches of a tree

Or a dead bird continuing to glide

Your howl persists despite the arrow piercing your chest
VOICE ONE, this is when I begin to love the blurred
image I have of sound

.... --- .-- .-.. --. -- --- .-. . --- -.- - .... .-. - .... --- .-- .-.. .. -. --.
.--. .-.. . .- ... . --..--

.- blue -.-. .... .- -. -. . .-.. . -.. repertoire of moan
You in the darkness of your howl as if trapped in a spurious
painting
An epiglottis of fear

The moon howls at you too with the voice of a defunct comet

.-   .... --- .-- .-..

.-   .... --- .-- .-..

A howl

-.. --- -   -.. .- ... .   -.. --- -   -.. --- -   -.. --- -   -.. .- ... .   -.. .- ... .   -.. .- ... .
-.. --- -   -.. .- ... .   -.. .- ... .   -.. --- -   -.. .- ... .   -.. --- -   -.. --- -

Furthermore

..-. ..- .-. - .... . .-. -- --- .-. .

you spawn all night
tuning teeth

-.. --- -   -.. .- ... .   -.. --- -   -.. --- -   -.. --- -   -.. .- ... .   -.. .- ... .   -.. .- ... .
-.. --- -   -.. .- ... .   -.. .- ... .   -.. --- -   -.. .- ... .   -.. --- -   -.. --- -

-.. --- -. -

.-.. . -

-.. --- -. -   -- .

.-.. . -   ... .-.. . . .--.

-- .   -.. --- -. -

... .-.. . . .--.   .-- .- -.-- .

-.. --- -. -   -- .

.-- .- -.-- .
-- .

..- .--.

don't

let

me

sleep

don't
wake
me
up

Eros

Lift a man's skirts with a straw
and watch the winter ryegrass

swell as if to reveal the incense leap
below the netherworld of manhood

You forgot the reedy smell of infancy

and became
a flammable herb
wilting in the lift
of a man's skirts

His hoary gasp grew tillers

Eat his hair his face
Steal his need

They call it the Great Sickness for
chilled deviled pants don't sleep

Bone Diary

In the fractured dark
the sacrilege of
thighs   A fear of

my smell   The blood
flowing down

the groin   It touches
the left and right inner thigh
rouge on leg cheek, a paltry wound
a rub   all animals can see now
me

My reliquary flows deep

and reeks of daubed dirt

"I am not my blood"

"I am not an estranged maternal gift"

My boyhood shaped
as rainfall inside cell

a mute rune
Fed it to the pigs
and porcupines

All directions lead back here
minutes sting
i.e. they loop around as suicidal wasps

hoisting a queer
new face eternal in return

their immortality minus your death
i.e. if my ghost testicles could sing…

(shrunken little
elves still in their
birth cocoon)

words get lost in the haze

"to the nearest you, this empty painting"

The face got lost
in the crowd

The patter in the rain not witnessed

"a single immobile sparrow" the cow, only

For hours I abstained from thinking about time

i.e. minutes seized
my boy parts

Then in the
epicenter
of a tree,

a condemned man

feet,
on branches

Collect body
parts in
chilled

amphora,
a mother will
pour along

her reflection
So is a bonfire
to a woman's feet

a pithos to
a naked body

Divine suction
in cracking ice

Parasites
depart thru
nostrils, dried
pollen of dirt

A mirage is a drupe
approaching mouth

While at first
birds are hailed

A few days
buzzing songs

every time one
thinks to think

All words for fire
flooding down

preempting robustly
chewing on taproots

My sauvignon hair
brittle, with all the

ugliness of daylight
excuse a mountain

for staying out of
all shades of light

No contemplation

Banded snow
in this dubious hour

As, they say
"already"

a roe among slayers
necktie of Sargasso weed

Consider the oath taken
before a judge or an altar

the bend of the head
and preceding silence

when the inventory
of my secrets swirls

Beast for regress

I won't speak its scraping angles

As,
leave the bodily

to me

for it will continue

to aggregate

The sound of oxygen brittle burning
in the throat is not my throat Gasp

Follows augury, heirloom
of hades
My poverty drips witchy wet
gloom

In my father's garden I first became
my father's son and swallowed thick

seed, a momentous heretical error,
i.e. the truth defamed by resin lips

Suddenly I'm blind, then I remember:
I don't want to see my body

or this lupine sun

My Adam's apple forgets to be,
quivers with a strange muffled voice

I do not imitate who I am

As, insomnia: a vervain bed

When specks of morning entered the body

felt unprecedented

thinness   The bile
inside of sediment in skin

The blood is vast   Even when
wars have ended

The grasses weep

[*time has been bruised to the walls of this cell*   *and sponges to a secret nook*   *or vein*]

For the morning of
obscured origin is
fastidious

Sucking dancing spiracles
of beetle brain
A passerine soup
of white-throated dipper
w/ red bean apple sauce

Founded this clan
of wasps   Walked
impermanency
Bathed in lonely waters
by the devil's
fists

For road with roods
a barefooted kneel
coated with mud

In my father's garden I first
became
my father's son and swallowed thick

seed, a momentous heretical error,
i.e. the truth defamed by resin lips

As,
bending of twine   knees are stones   bones of hammers

As,
glutton ghosts

I drove the stake
to the ground,
you drive it into
me

The warden is a
ghost we forget
inside a closet

Jeanne's S~~on~~g

I feel the agony of a shut death
Earth ripped my human shreds
Insomnia is a soft ~~vervain~~ bed

~~Teach me a dog's meekness to~~
Be a lone whispery woodland
I feel the ~~agony~~ of a ~~shut~~ death

Cliff as ~~hot~~ wondrous eyelid I'm
Seasoned for the ~~tempting~~ leap
Insomnia is a lost vervain bed

Pant of fire becomes stead
Noon lands with ~~clawed~~ fervor
I feel the agony of a gut death

Insect nook in juggled leaf
Living off its bug wet-keef
~~Insomnia~~ is a soft vervain bed

My statue bends to noir
Steeple of drugged regret
I feel the agony of a shut death
Insomnia is a soft vervain ~~bed~~

"To avoid the unpalatable consequences of unidimensional time travel—the celebrated paradoxes of preventing one's own birth, etc.—it is reasonable to appeal instead to the theory of the multiverse. Rather than having a time traveler, S, journey into the past of his own universe (call it X) and thereby court the apparent contradictions, we can instead posit an alternative universe (P) as his proper destination. The event of S's departing the year 2001 for the year 1001 (say) will therefore be more precisely described as S's leaving his own universe and time, 2001X, and travelling not to 1001X, the ancestor of his own time, but rather to 1001P, i.e., the year 1001 in another universe. Any action S undertakes after travelling to the past occurs in an alternative universe and so cannot affect—and, a fortiori, contradict—the events of his own."

– John Abbruzzese

Biography

is a leaking vase
with holes where insects sleep

a pogrom The vase topples

and breaks each shard a grave
combusting
The vase is what
a woman looks like
as a pregnant boy

"The asterisk in the question mark is posthumous"

My biography a hornbeam sculpture

I scratch my name off its inscription

Now a beige
wedged curve
chiseled by
bear claws
Sprinkled
flies leave
their
pocked
marks
on dusty furniture
a hexed synthesis

The jug's holes
respire
Exhalation
is shadow

[*Rewind two hours, turn left on the hour*]

On the underside
of breath

an anti-chronology

rowing back from the end

My sex
peeled
to its
minimal
form

A hole (in a jug) you may bathe it
on Sunday after mass

(that frail smelly skin)

A still stone also

exemplifies

place
without
gaze

[*Fast forward however long you choose then hold your breath (5m)*]

This boy's hips

can't squeeze between two trees

Too wide for rabid sunshine

Their eggplant

lines
like unpeopled

runes

a swatch of emptiness

My pants rub

tightly
where the
boy's fetus

hits the bellybutton

[*Loop into a minute's swirl*]

Remember:
an arrowed
coffin spits
back a dead
body's light

[*Rewind in place over lunar drawing (incalculable)*]

I forgot to   own up to   my pale   mortality

choosing   the larval   instead

Place me   inside an   orifice of   time, any

cavity   will   do

[*Its tree-like appearance being deceptive & dangerous, peel a minute into a simmer*]

The crown of thorns you

waved to reel

me in trekking

a verb in
which my face

was written
elked with froth
battered as a mushy

grape I began to see in lieu of rain
drops
settling like

pinched spider webs
secondary
to the afterlife in which I spin

as garment of light
one step ahead of
my old body
forming its
stormy shadow,

you can see
it under

[this
blue
bulb]

[*Pick a minute and taste its pawed acidity (1m)*]

As,

stones
are
made
for
creeping
also
words
in my
white
cross
lick this
weedy
soul

[*Two auscultations per second (1s)*]

sparrow is
the length
I need
I hear
abraded
squeals of
looming
prisoners
"do you
prefer a
morning
or an
evening
death?"
"three
a.m. like
the trinity,
hourly &
foolish
as a pup"

[*Of the second complicity in hours (too soon to tell)*]

Somethi
ng to
dunk my
eye,
sir" "I
made it
this far
w/out
fear" "for
blood's
my
vinegar
& I'm
dolloped
w/fire
like an
Easter
newlywe
d

[*Start counting backward from zero*]

I see better now with this altered

body

A Dream

last night barely at the edge of a dream & finding the glowing triad
of your name, Jeanne d'Arc
          [trees older than time fleshing your face with leaves]
last night liquescent spreading cloud-to-cloud [& you breathing
mammoth dreams unprepared for
          osmotic fire]
last night ordinary plums, Jeanne, inside sacks of wheat loomed like
elastic elephants
[commotion
          of saccades in your buttoned sleep]
last night I slept in your saga as clenched fist [Domrémy-la-Pucelle
          palpitated, remember its juicy green? its lone oranges? its
          cosseted weeds?]
[for] last night olfaction became factoid looping the circular in trees
          [I suspected a fluttering fist]
last night you sat between eggs while the sun corroded udders
last night peril traveled the length of your ulna arriving ulcery and
          ulpic [arriving before its time in urn or uloid boxes, arriving
          ululant or umbered]
[for] last night only you could have ridden those horses
[for] last night only you could have bathed those mules
last night I slept in the lachrymal basin that haunts your dreams [&
          the muddy water smelled like milk]
last night [did you wake up to a morning's neigh speckled with
          future fishes, with future figs & firs, with future fires &
          foes?]
last night did it appear again? sarcophagi suggesting mountain
last night as if the eelpout choked a tender portion of your dream
          & you were left with its brine & skin, you were left with its
          coiling swing
last night I slept wrapped in meat
last night as if I knew the face you carry now

Hearsay About Jeanne d'Arc

"That this woman is a liar & a witch"
"That her cohorts nest with adders"

"That she bows to a makeshift king"
"That her gloved claws are dark sin"

"That she speaks with slurring tongues"
"That she does not kill but watches die"

"That her banner's flesh is bocasin white"
"That her piglets groan, her sparrows croak"

"That she whispers widowhood"
& clings to morphine chains"

"That her lizard mouth trembles with jeers"
"That she eats the broth of marrow"

"That her cobalt eyes command armies of spiders"
"That her ribbons hide deadly nests of wasps"

"That her strength equals two men & an axe"
"That she can lift mares with her feet"

"That her left hand knows secrets her right conceals"
"That she has seen auroras white as summer clouds"

"That she birthed a centaur"
"That the centaur is her helper"

"That he lays in her bed
& their children are their slaves"

"That she traps unicorns in a circle of fire"
"That she boils their meat, dries their bones

on boulders, sharpens their femurs, slices
the skulls of sinners with their sharp points,

eats their meat & bathes in their blood
wears their ears round her neck & keeps

the horns tucked on her belt
to ward off mountain lions."

"That she shifts beehives with her fists"
& ties men's tongues with her thoughts"

"That she learned the alphabet in a dream"
& scrawls the script of god on her horse's skin"

"That she burns her forehead each morning"
& slaps her arms with a switch caked in salt"

"That she drinks only water & eats only bread
at noon with her cheek lapping the earthworm."

"That her fangled teeth tear through living deer"
"That she pulls the gizzards from birds with her bare hands"

"That she doesn't sleep or goes to church
or blinks her eyes or turns her neck or flares

her nostrils or moves her lips or tosses her head
her arms & legs move so fast they stand still."

"That she gorges herself on liver"
"That she doesn't eat garlic or salt"

"That she copulates like an old harpy"
"That she serves the forest nymphs"

"That her belly is covered in fur"
"That her teeth are moldy & gray"

"That a cicada gurgles in her throat"
"That she's pagan as brazen rouge"

"That the fox avoids her & the hare suppresses her"
"That the swan fears her & the mallard attacks her"

"That her looks weave fatal spells:
the virgins swoon, the boys repent"

"That wheat wilts where she
walked & oaks begin to burn"

"That lilies grow in her footsteps
& loons sing where her body laid"

"That her face is a bright red coral"
"That her body is a darkwater spell"

"That she'll spike you with her trident"
"For she's a rain-filled spook"

"That she drives the hatchet to the heart"
"That she cups your blood in her palms"

"That her saffron hair smells of midnight"
"That her rabbit hands prickle like fins"

"That her baying brain swats distances"
"& her eyes are two Phrygian wounds"

30 May 1431
(Morse Code)

look @ me
wrathfully
spacious lyke
a city w/out
people

u & eye
are the
same, people

look @ my
burnt scalp
black nails
is fire's
minions

toes in r.i.p.
faked by royalty
twittering for
roomy-self

"Not a metaphor for your death
Or cipher of your mortality."

Jeanne d'Arc to Carl Dreyer

Notes

Most of the French text featured in "Understanding" was taken verbatim from the original transcript of Joan of Arc's trial and the time cues correspond to intertitles or scenes in Carl Dreyer's film.

The quotation in the first intertitle (p. 5), "Militarism is the compulsory, universal use of violence as a means to the ends of the state," is taken from Walter Benjamin's "Critique of Violence."

www.ingramcontent.com/pod-product-compliance
Lightning Source LLC
Chambersburg PA
CBHW032047290426
44110CB00012B/995
* 9 7 8 0 6 9 2 1 5 0 2 9 0 *